TREVOR HUDSON

# Pauses

## *for*

# Pentecost

—

## 50 Words for Easter People

UPPER
ROOM BOOKS®
NASHVILLE

PAUSES FOR PENTECOST: 50 WORDS FOR EASTER PEOPLE
Copyright © 2017 by Trevor Hudson
All rights reserved.

Upper Room Books® website: books.upperroom.org

Upper Room®, Upper Room Books®, and design logos are trademarks owned by The Upper Room®, Nashville, Tennessee. All rights reserved.

All scripture quotations, unless otherwise indicated, are taken from the Holy Bible, New International Version®, NIV®. Copyright ©1973, 1978, 1984, 2011 by Biblica, Inc.™ Used by permission of Zondervan. All rights reserved worldwide. www.zondervan.com

Scripture quotations marked NRSV are from the New Revised Standard Version Bible, copyright © 1989 National Council of the Churches of Christ in the United States of America. Used by permission. All rights reserved.

Cover design, illustration, and interior design: Faceout Studio
Cover image: Shutterstock

Print ISBN: 978-0-8358-1763-9
Mobi ISBN: 978-0-8358-1764-6
Epub ISBN: 978-0-8358-1765-3

Printed in the United States of America

For Bill Meaker,
a dear friend who has over the years
helped me so much with my writing efforts

# Contents

## Fourth Week of Eastertide

## Fifth Week of Eastertide

## Sixth Week of Eastertide

## Seventh Week of Eastertide

# INTRODUCTION

As followers of Christ, we are invited to become Easter people filled with God's Spirit. The Resurrection is the life-giving center of our faith. Without it there would not be a Christian story, a Christian church, or a Christian spirituality. Certainly there would be no Ascension or Pentecost to celebrate. The Resurrection event proclaims that Christ lives beyond crucifixion, validates as true his teachings about how to live in the kingdom of God, and reveals that his cross was indeed not a defeat but a victory of God's self-giving love over all the destructive powers of sin and death. Turning from our old ways of life and becoming linked in faith with the risen Jesus today is to experience a greater fullness of life wherever we are. This is the astonishing, amazing good news of our faith.

Wonderfully, there is a time set aside in the Christian calendar for us to enter more fully into this good news. It has traditionally been called Eastertide, or the Easter Season. Eastertide refers to those fifty days from Easter Sunday to the Day of Pentecost. In the early church's calendar, Eastertide represented the middle of the church year. In this season, we follow the risen Christ and his encounters with his disciples up to that moment when he ascends to his Father, and then we wait for ten days until his Spirit is poured out on them. We could say that the resurrection of Jesus finds its glorious fulfillment in the sending of the Holy Spirit at Pentecost. Hence the combination of Easter and Pentecost themes in the title of this little book: *Pauses for Pentecost: 50 Words for Easter People.*

Easter is also a season that many Christians have forgotten! Certainly our surrounding consumeristic culture does not know what to do with it. Somehow, Resurrection and Pentecost cannot be packaged, consumed, or marketed. As a result, we often limit our engagement with this extraordinary season to Easter Sunday Communion, perhaps an Ascension worship service forty days later, and then ten days after that a Pentecost Sunday celebration. When have we ever taken all these fifty days to consciously and deliberately walk the path from the Resurrection to Pentecost? In my conversations with others, I have discovered very few who do.

We are all the poorer for this neglect. The days between Jesus' resurrection and the giving of his Spirit are filled with his unseen presence, available to those who love him in a new and powerful way. Similarly, if we are willing to take the time to pause, Eastertide can punctuate this time for us with precious encounters with our risen Lord. Each time he comes to his disciples, whether in one of those resurrection encounters or in the power of his Holy Spirit, he provides for the special needs of an individual or a group. In the same way, he comes to us to console and to challenge us as we open ourselves to him.

In this little book, I am interested in exploring how we can live today as Easter people filled with God's Spirit. How do we live, in the midst of our relationships and daily work, a life permeated by the present companionship of the risen and ascended Jesus? What does it mean to be genuinely empowered by his Spirit in a world characterized by painful divisions, immeasurable human suffering, and the relentless devastation of creation itself? How do we respond and react to bad news, both personal and social, in a world in which God has raised

Christ from the dead? In a nutshell, I want us to discover how we can cultivate an Easter imagination and practice a Pentecost life where we are.

Here is how I suggest we go about doing this. First, let us joyfully claim Eastertide as one of God's special time-gifts. Along with Advent and Lent, let us make sure that this neglected season finds its rightful place in our Christian calendar. As we have seen, it will draw us into the crucial events of Jesus' resurrection and ascension, as well as the gift of the Pentecost experience. Let us commit ourselves to walk through this time day by day so that we may experience what it really means to live as Easter people empowered by the breath of the Holy Spirit.

Second, I've complied fifty biblical words to help us reimagine our lives as Easter people filled with God's Spirit. These words will come from scriptural passages that will draw us into our risen lives with Christ. I hope that they will point us toward that vivid aliveness, ever-increasing joy, and inner freedom that the early disciples experienced as they encountered Jesus in his resurrected presence and in his Spirit. Certainly the remarkable changes that we see in their lives, after the crucifixion left them hopeless and despairing, bear a convincing witness to the transforming reality of the Resurrection, Ascension, and Pentecost events.

Third, along with a daily meditation on each word, I suggest fifty different daily practices. Please know that these practices will not demand much extra time. Involving simple daily intentions and actions, they are designed to let the new life of the Resurrection and the power of Pentecost flow into our messy lives and broken relationships. Often we find ourselves in life situations where hopelessness and despair rob us of our joy and delight. Life becomes heavy, and we feel overwhelmed and despondent. Often a simple spiritual intention or practice, entered into with simple trust in the risen Christ, brings us alive again with the special kind of aliveness we see in those early disciples at the Resurrection and Pentecost.

Lastly, I invite you to get together with some friends with whom you can go through this book. Perhaps you can commit to meeting once a week for seven weeks. Begin with a prayer, inviting God to be present, and then let each person share his or her experience of the week's meditations and practices. Pay special attention to the meditation and practice that were most helpful for each person. Foster a safe space for sharing by keeping confidential what group members share, and try not to correct other persons when you think they are not doing it right. Remember that becoming Easter people in the power of the Spirit is a shared journey.

In closing, my Eastertide hope for you is that by walking along the path of the Resurrection toward Pentecost, you will be led more deeply into the exhilarating fullness of life promised to us by Jesus. I pray that the joy of the risen Christ will surprise you and fill you with the energy of his Spirit. Here is a prayer that you can pray as you begin the journey:

*Lord Jesus Christ, breathe the freshness of your Spirit into us that we may come alive again to the possibilities and potential of our own lives, to the uniqueness and wonder of each person around us, to the beauty and brutality of our world, and most especially to the wondrous glory of God that fills our universe. May we truly become Easter people filled with your Spirit!*

# STONE

*After the Sabbath, at dawn on the first day of the week,*
*Mary Magdalene and the other Mary went to look at the tomb.*
*There was a violent earthquake,*
*for an angel of the Lord came down from heaven and,*
*going to the tomb, rolled back the stone and sat on it.*
**Matthew 28:1-2**

Eastertide is all about coming alive to the mystery of our own existence, to the uniqueness and sacredness of those around us, to the unearned gifts of creation that bless us each day, and to the wondrous presence of God that fills all things. The resurrected Jesus invites each of us to rise up into the fullness of our lives. Right at the beginning of this journey, we need to remind ourselves that this is the good news the risen Christ wants us to experience.

But first, as we are reminded today in our Gospel reading, those stones blocking this newness of life need to be rolled away. I wonder what your particular stone may look like right now. Think for a moment about the biblical picture of us having "hearts of stone" (Zech. 7:12). Hearts of stone are hardened, cold, and unresponsive. When our hearts are hard, we want little to do with God. We lack a sense of wonder, awe, and reverence. We struggle to love unselfishly. Everything to do with our faith and our lives feels dull and bland and gray.

Stony hearts can express themselves in even more destructive ways. Sometimes we find ourselves judging others negatively when they mess up rather than seeking to understand their situations more fully. Or we think that we are better than others or superior to them and end up living with deadly self-righteousness. Sometimes our hearts become hard with a refusal to forgive or with resentment or with bitterness or even with destructive hatred. There may also exist stones of grief, failure, negativity, cynicism, guilt, and the list continues. The terrible thing about these stones is how they obstruct our access to the life God wants to give us.

Eastertide is the season for our hearts of stone to become hearts of flesh again, filled with the Spirit. Spirit-filled hearts are aware and warm and responsive. The good news is this: Jesus wants to meets us in the power of his Spirit that we may come alive again to the presence of God, to ourselves, to others, and to all creation!

### *Daily Practice*

Go outside and pick up a stone. Let it represent whatever it is that stops you from living fully. If you are able, write on it one word describing the stone in your heart. Offer it to God with the request that God will help you roll it away. Then throw the stone as far as you can.

# ANGEL

*His appearance was like lightning,*
*and his clothes were white as snow.*
*The guards were so afraid of him that they shook*
*and became like dead men.*

*The angel said to the women, "Do not be afraid,*
*for I know that you are looking for Jesus,*
*who was crucified. He is not here;*
*he has risen, just as he said.*
**Matthew 28:3-6**

Thankfully, we are not left alone to roll away those stones that keep us from coming alive again. Our Resurrection story tells us that God sends us an angel to help us move them away. Notice everything that the angel does in our Gospel reading. Besides rolling away the stone, the angel also helps the women at the empty tomb to grasp what has happened. The angel explains to them that what Jesus had said to them about his overcoming death has come true. They are indeed witnesses to the good news of the Resurrection. Jesus is alive again!

Let us think a bit more about angels. On the one hand, they sometimes come to us in a very human way. They may come in the form of a loved one with whom we can talk about those stones that harden our hearts, as a good friend who keeps encouraging us to reach out for new life, or as a stranger who enters our life unexpectedly with wisdom and insight that shed light on our darkness. These people act for us as messengers from God who bring resurrection hope into our deadness.

On the other hand, angels from the Lord may come in a more spiritual way. They may appear in a significant dream that lights up an obstacle that prevents us from living fully, in a wide-awake vision that strengthens us to do what we need to do, or in a surprise thought that pops into our minds, suggesting possibilities that we had not thought of before. Sometimes the angel may come to us in the words of a Gospel reading like the Eastertide verses we are thinking about now.

However angels of the Resurrection appear to us, they always help us to understand more deeply the good news, just as the angel did with the women at the empty tomb. Jesus is now the Risen One, available and reaching out to each of us in the power of his Spirit, desiring to bring us alive again in a new way!

### *Daily Practice*

Ask God to help you become more aware of angels in your life. Reflect on the past day and ask yourself, *Was there a moment today when I experienced life and light and hope touching me in my darkness?* Thank God for this experience, and be on the lookout for an angelic encounter each day.

# AHEAD

*"Then go quickly and tell his disciples:*
*'He has risen from the dead and*
*is going ahead of you into Galilee.*
*There you will see him.' Now I have told you."*
**Matthew 28:7**

Where are you going in the next few hours? Our Galilee represents what we are moving toward. Maybe you are getting ready to see a client, to attend an important business meeting, to visit a good friend, to pick up your child from school, or to visit a loved one in the hospital. Whatever your Galilee may look like, wherever you may be going today, Christ goes ahead of you and promises to meet you there. This is the good news of the Resurrection!

When this Easter reality grasps our hearts and minds, it radically shapes how we enter each new situation in our lives. We begin to say to ourselves, *Christ is already present where I am going. I will not be on my own. I do not have to depend on my own resources of knowledge and competence alone. While I will do my very best in this situation, I will not only trust my best but I will also trust him.* Do you feel the difference this brings?

This good news also keeps us living on tiptoe in every new situation. Because Christ has already arrived there, we cultivate a certain curiosity. We begin to wonder, *What is he doing? What is he saying? How is he creating another little Easter story in this place? How can we join him in the resurrection work that he is doing right now? What do we need to say and do to become partners with his Spirit in bringing new life?* Ordinary life becomes filled with possibilities of surprising resurrection encounters.

Just as the angel promises those women at the empty tomb that the risen Jesus will go ahead into Galilee, so he goes before us to meet us in whatever situation may represent our Galilee. When we recognize his presence and respond to him, resurrection happens in the midst of our daily lives. This is what it means to live today as Easter people filled with the Holy Spirit.

### *Daily Practice*

Imagine the next situation into which you will enter. Nurture the sense of expectancy and anticipation in your heart and mind. Ask Christ to help you to recognize what he is doing there and to help you with his Spirit to respond through your words and actions.

# JOY

*The women hurried away from the tomb,*
*afraid yet filled with joy, and ran to tell his disciples.*
**Matthew 28:8**

Eastertide is a time for us to open our hearts and minds more widely to the joy of God. These women at the tomb, frightened as they are by the events that have taken place, are nonetheless filled with joy. The joy of the risen Christ has pervaded their whole beings. Somehow they now know deep down that, because of what has taken place in the empty tomb, ultimately all will be well.

Fullness of joy characterizes Easter people. Remember Jesus' promises to his disciples on the night before his crucifixion: "I have told you this so that my joy may be in you and that your joy may be complete" (John 15:11). When we are full of joy, life really becomes worth living. Full joy is, as Dallas Willard has written, our first line of defense against weakness, failure, and disease of mind and body.* Even when these things do break into our lives, "the joy of the Lord is your strength" (Neh. 8:10).

How do we open ourselves to this resurrection joy? Certainly we cannot manufacture it for ourselves. It can only be produced in our lives by the Spirit of Christ himself. This does not mean we sit back and do nothing. It is always our responsibility to continually focus our hearts and minds—not on our past failures or sins, on our future concerns and worries, or on those ever-present struggles that come our way each day but on

*Dallas Willard, *Renovation of the Heart: Putting On the Character of Christ* (Colorado Springs: NavPress, 2006).

the God who raised Jesus from the dead. As we choose to do this with simple trust, the Holy Spirit will impart greater measures of divine joy into our lives.

There can be no greater joy than knowing that nothing, not even death, can ever separate us from the love that God has for us in Jesus Christ. (See Romans 8:38-39.) Will you choose to open yourself more deeply to this joy today?

### *Daily Practice*

Spend a few moments quietly worshiping God. Praise God for the mighty work that God did in raising Jesus from the grave. Repeat and memorize Psalm 92:4: "For you make me glad by your deeds, LORD; I sing for joy at what your hands have done."

# CRYING

*[Jesus] asked her, "Woman, why are you crying?*
*Who is it you are looking for?"*
**John 20:15**

In his telling of the early Easter-morning encounter, John describes Mary as heartbroken. She has gone to the tomb hoping to give Jesus her last act of love by anointing his body. To her great distress, the stone has been rolled away, and the body of Jesus is gone. She is overcome with anguish and heartache. Not being able to perform the final ritual is the last straw for her. She has come to the end of her rope.

It is exactly at this point, at the end of her rope, that the risen Jesus comes to her. This is always where he comes to us. He encounters us in our heartache and heartbreak and asks us the same question he asks Mary: "Why are you crying?" Like Mary, we need to hear this question and respond to it. To avoid this question is to run away from our pain, and the consequences of this often can be numerous and harmful. We need to express pain and help it find its voice in order to heal.

I wonder how you would respond to Jesus' question, *Why are you crying?* Mary answers, "They have taken my Lord away, . . . and I don't know where they have put him" (John 20:13). She enters into honest conversation with Jesus about her pain. Slowly, she recognizes that the One with her is indeed Jesus, now wonderfully and gloriously alive. This can be our experience too. When we take Jesus' question seriously and share our response aloud with him, we too may come to experience his risen presence in the midst of our tears.

Easter people know what it means to cry. They also have personally come to know that one very important activity of the Spirit is to help us experience the risen Christ in the midst of our tears. May this be part of our Eastertide experience as well.

### *Daily Practice*

Experiment with your imagination in prayer today. Go with Mary to the tomb. Stand with her as she weeps. Watch the risen Jesus come and ask her his question. Listen to Mary as she answers. Now Jesus turns to you and asks you the same question. Respond to him from your heart. Listen to and watch for his response.

# BURNING

*They asked each other,*
*"Were not our hearts burning within us*
*while he talked with us on the road*
*and opened the Scriptures to us?"*
**Luke 24:32**

Many know this beautiful Gospel scene well. Two heartbroken disciples are on their way home to Emmaus from Jerusalem. They have run out of hope. The One they thought was the Messiah has been crucified. While they walk, the risen Jesus joins them and enters into conversation with them. They invite him home, break bread with him, and they recognize him. When he vanishes from their sight, they speak excitedly about how they had felt their hearts burning within them while he spoke with them on the road. Suddenly, they have a new and hope-filled view of life.

This personal meeting with the risen Jesus is available to all who feel hopeless. He comes to each one of us through his Spirit, walks alongside us, and desires to enter into conversation with us. He wants to know about the dark thoughts and feelings in our hearts. He opens our minds to words of scripture so that they speak directly and personally to our situations. He makes himself known to us as bread is broken and wine is poured. In moments like these, our hearts also begin to burn again with new faith and hope and love.

However, none of this happens without our involvement. Like those two early disciples, our invisible Companion invites us to enter into conversation, sharing with him our inner agony and anguish. We must open the doors of our lives and homes to his resurrected presence. We too are to share in the bread and wine that he offers to his gathered people. Above all, we also need to learn how to listen to his voice, especially in the biblical story, shedding light on what we are going through and warming our hearts with his words of truth and new perspectives.

Easter people know that Jesus is alive, he lives beyond crucifixion, and through his Spirit he offers us in our hopelessness the gift of his healing presence and word. May our eyes also be opened to recognize Jesus in our midst so that our hearts may burn within us!

### *Daily Practice*

Take a short walk today. Keep the Emmaus story in your mind. Ask the risen Christ to be your Companion. As you stroll along your own Emmaus road, bring a problem that you are facing to him. Think of your favorite scripture story and let it confront what you are going through. Listen to what the Spirit may be saying to you.

# TABLE

*When [Jesus] was at the table with them,*
*he took bread, gave thanks,*
*broke it and began to give it to them.*
**Luke 24:30**

Have you ever noticed how many times in Luke's Gospel Jesus sits around the table for a meal? He regularly shared meals with others, whether they are Pharisees, sinners and tax collectors, or his disciples. We learn more of what he teaches about his heavenly Parent on these occasions than from what he says in the synagogue. Meals at the table are some of Jesus' favorite settings for him to make visible to others the good news of God's mercy and acceptance of all people.

Not surprisingly, it is while they are having a meal around a table with the Stranger they had met on the road that those two Emmaus pilgrims experience the resurrection presence of Jesus. Recall that Gospel moment one more time. The two of them have walked several miles. They are tired and hungry. After Jesus joins them, they invite him into their home. There they sit around the table with him. While they are eating, Jesus suddenly becomes the host. He takes bread, gives thanks, breaks it, and gives it to them. In that moment, they recognize him.

Mealtimes around the table can also become resurrection moments for us. These are the down-to-earth, sacred moments when we come together with others, share what is on our hearts, listen to one another, and enjoy a meal. Moments like these keep us in touch with those close to us, renew special friendships, and help strangers feel welcome. These are times of connection and celebration and hospitality. But they are also more than all these things. They also create the needed space for us to experience the risen One, surprising us and touching our lives with his love and care as we eat, drink, and talk with one another.

Next time you sit down together with others for a meal, be expectant and open. It may just be that Jesus makes another resurrection appearance at your table!

### *Daily Practice*

When you sit down at the table today to share a meal, keep your inner eyes open for how Christ may be present. If you usually eat alone, invite someone to join you around the table.

# BREATHED

*And with that [Jesus] breathed on them and said,*
*"Receive the Holy Spirit."*
**John 20:22**

This moment must be one of the most intimate and intense in the New Testament. Imagine the scene behind locked doors. Fear fills the air. Jesus, standing in the midst of his disciples, breathes on them and gives them the gift of his own personal breath. This is the breath by which he has lived and loved and spoken. Yet his breath is also the Holy Spirit, our heavenly Parent's special gift and presence that Jesus has promised will be given to his disciples. Breath, in Jesus' mind, is much more than a symbol for the Spirit. When he breathes onto and into his disciples, he is giving them the actual presence of his own Spirit.

Now, think of your own breath for a moment. It symbolizes a lot about your life. The Catholic scholar Raniero Cantalamessa has written that our breath signifies what is most inward and intimate, most vital and most personal about us.* Our breath keeps us alive. This is why feeling suffocated terrifies us. "I can't breathe," we cry out, "I need air." If people look as if they are going to faint or they begin to panic or they feel totally overwhelmed, we say to them, "Breathe. Take a deep breath." Nothing is more important to staying alive than breathing in and breathing out.

*Raniero Cantalamessa, *Come, Creator Spirit: Meditations on the Veni Creator* (Pretoria, South Africa: Protea Book House, 2003), 20.

The comparisons to our lives with God are obvious. At the very least, there are times when our souls cry out for air. We feel suffocated by fears and anxieties, exhausted by our stresses and strains. Facing these challenges and crises, we feel out of breath. We wonder whether our winded lives can keep going. At the very worst, sometimes our souls literally die because of our neglect or our sin. Sometimes it is a painful grief that sucks the life out of us. Wonderfully, Ezekiel's vision of God's Breath entering dead bones and giving them life reminds us that the Spirit always brings life again into the graveyards of our lives. (See Ezekiel 37:1-14.)

Easter people know that taking deep breaths of the Holy Spirit must become a daily habit. The good news is that the risen Jesus continues to breathe on and into us. He is willing to do this for anyone and everyone, especially for those willing to come close enough to feel his breath.

### *Daily Practice*

Pay attention to your breathing today. Imagine when you inhale that you are breathing the Spirit of God into your whole being. When you exhale, imagine that you are breathing out the love of Christ into the world around you.

# DOUBT

*[Jesus] said to Thomas,*
*"Put your finger here; see my hands.*
*Reach out your hand and put it into my side.*
*Stop doubting and believe."*
**John 20:27**

Most of us experience doubt in our journeys with God at one time or another. Doubt enters our lives through many different doorways. It could be through repeated disappointment, unanswered prayer, or an intellectual struggle with the reality of the invisible realm. For many of us, however, it is through the doorway of suffering that doubt enters. Our own suffering, the suffering of a loved one, or immeasurable pain in the world around us can affect our faith. Right now, you may be struggling with doubt.

Thomas represents those of us whose faith has been shaken by doubt. His story shows us that when we acknowledge our doubt honestly, it can lead us into a deeper faith. Read about him again in John's Gospel. (See John 20:24-29.) Notice how Jesus reaches out to help Thomas believe. There is no condemnation whatsoever. Rather, as we see in today's verse, Jesus offers Thomas evidence that encourages him to move beyond his doubt. Eventually, Thomas takes his step of faith and confesses before Jesus, "My Lord and my God" (John 20:28).

Obviously we are not given the same powerful evidence that Thomas receives. But many experiences help us move beyond our doubt. First, we live in a world of overwhelming beauty and intricate structure that nothing produced by human beings can match. Then, there is our own experience of ourselves, our sense of right or wrong, that invites explanation. Most of all, there is the radical change that happens in those early disciples after the Crucifixion. Something must have happened to transform their fear into boldness, their despair into hope, their disbelief into trust. How else can we explain it?

None of these reasons give us total proof. However, they do bring us to what Kallistos Ware calls "the threshold of faith."* Like Thomas, we too need to take the step of faith. And when we do, we will discover the reality of Christ present and alive in our own experience.

### *Daily Practice*

Write down your own confession of faith in Jesus today. Use your own words, not Thomas's words. What are the words or images that come into your mind when you think of the meaning of Jesus for yourself? After you have done this, take Thomas's words with you into the day and repeat them as often as you can.

*Kallistos Ware, *The Orthodox Way* (Crestwood, NY: St. Vladimir's Seminary Press, 1979), 21.

# MORNING

*Early in the morning, Jesus stood on the shore,*
*but the disciples did not realize that it was Jesus.*
**John 21:4**

Are you a morning person? Our experiences differ greatly. Some of us love greeting the new day. We receive it with joy and are filled with a sense of eager expectation. We cannot wait to get going with the tasks and responsibilities that await us. Some take a bit longer to get going. Others wake up with a sense of heaviness and fatigue. We wonder how we are going to make it through the day, especially on those gray mornings when it is difficult to get out of bed. Let me ask you: How did you feel first thing this morning?

As this special Easter morning dawns, the disciples are deeply despondent. They have been out fishing all night but have caught nothing. All their efforts have been fruitless. Then as the darkness of the night gives way to the rising of the sun, they catch a glimpse of a figure standing on the shore, waiting for them. At first they do not realize that it is Jesus, but when he calls out and gives them fresh instructions about where to throw their nets, resulting in an amazing catch, they recognize him.

There is an Easter promise for all of us in this Gospel encounter. The risen Christ waits to personally meet us every new morning. Whether we wake up with feelings of joyful anticipation or with a sense of desolation and sadness, Jesus greets us by name and offers us direction for our day. Through the gift of his Spirit offered to each of us, he then wants to accompany us through whatever challenge and difficulty the day may hold for us. Indeed, as this story reminds us, we can be assured of his living presence reaching out to us, especially in those tasks where we have labored and seemingly have gotten nowhere.

Easter people start each morning knowing this assurance. We receive the day as a gift. We give thanks for it. We acknowledge the risen One who greets us. We listen for his voice. And then we seek to do whatever it is that he tells us to do.

### *Daily Practice*

Think about how you can develop a simple ritual around that moment when you open the curtains each morning. Perhaps as you draw them apart, you can simply say "Thank you," or "Lord, I greet you," "Jesus, have mercy," or another short phrase that expresses your resurrection hope for the day.

# LEAD

*"Very truly I tell you,*
*when you were younger you dressed yourself*
*and went where you wanted;*
*but when you are old you will stretch out your hands,*
*and someone else will dress you*
*and lead you where you do not want to go."*

**John 21:18**

The resurrection encounter between Jesus and Peter ends on a challenging note. After Jesus meets the disciples on the shore and shares fish and bread with them, he goes for a stroll with Peter. As they walk together, Jesus asks Peter three times whether he loves him. When Peter responds positively, Jesus commissions him with the task of shepherding his flock. Then Jesus prophesies that Peter will be led into a costly laying down of his life for others.

Following the risen Christ is not always about doing what we like. While there are most certainly moments when we can and must take the initiative in our discipleship, there are also times when we need to be led by Jesus. As it is for Peter, Jesus sometimes asks us to lay down our lives in specific and practical ways for others. But because we follow One who has defeated death, resurrection joy and life will always accompany this laying down of our lives for his sake. As Paul the apostle says, Jesus invites us to share both in the power of his resurrection and in the fellowship of his sufferings.

Jesus may lead us to lay down our lives for others in many different costly ways. We lay down our lives for others when we put aside our own concerns and listen attentively to another person's pain, when we look not only to our interests but also to the interests of those around us, when we go the extra mile in our efforts to assist materially someone in desperate need, when we give significant time to be with another person experiencing difficulty, and when we risk public criticism for supporting a just but unpopular cause on behalf of others. All these actions, and countless others, are examples of ways the Spirit calls us as Easter people.

I wonder how Jesus is calling you right now to lay down your life for the sake of others. As you respond—like Peter did—you too will reflect the heart of the Good Shepherd who gave his life for us all.

### *Daily Practice*

Pray to the Lord today: *Jesus, show me that you are leading me to lay my life down in the next few hours for someone in need.* Let him lead you into whatever it is that will bring care and concern to someone else.

# ALIVE

*Because of his great love for us,*
*God, who is rich in mercy,*
*made us alive with Christ*
*even when we were dead in transgressions—*
*it is by grace you have been saved.*
**Ephesians 2:4-5**

Are there moments when you feel more dead than alive? I am sure you know what I mean. To be alive is to be responsive to whatever is around us. It is to interact with people and circumstances in a way that is purposeful yet also joyfully spontaneous. I am always relieved when, on those occasions I go to see my doctor, my knee responds instinctively as she taps the nerve under my kneecap. With a smile she will usually say to me afterwards, "You are still alive!" Responsiveness characterizes the very essence of being alive.

By contrast, to be dead is to be nonresponsive. We all know what this is like. It is those empty times when we feel totally unresponsive to God, to the promptings of the Holy Spirit, to the words of scripture, and to prayer. We feel apathetic, uncaring, and indifferent in our relationships with those around us. Everything, including that which is beautiful and good, seems bland and boring. No longer are our everyday lives filled with a sense of childlike wonder and delight. We become the walking dead. It is a painful space in which to dwell.

As we can see from the verse above, Paul knows about this frightening deadness of spirit. But he has also come to know how we can be brought alive. For him "being dead in transgressions" is a spiritual malaise that is healed through an encounter with God's free grace and rich mercy, made available in Jesus Christ. His message is that, to put it bluntly, we must deal with God if we want to be raised into newness of life. God alone, the giver of life and the conqueror of death, can deliver us from our spiritual deadness. This happens as we turn toward the resurrected One, open ourselves to his life-giving breath, and courageously make choices for life, day after day.

Anglican writer John V. Taylor points out that God is not hugely concerned about whether we are religious or not. Rather, what matters to God—and matters supremely—is whether we are alive or not. How do you respond?

### *Daily Practice*

Make one choice for life today. It could be with regard to your own health of body and mind, a strained relationship, a difficult work situation, or a particular need in your community. Ask God to help you live your choice in the coming day.

# RAISED

*Since, then, you have been raised with Christ,*
*set your hearts on things above, where Christ is,*
*seated at the right hand of God.*
**Colossians 3:1**

Becoming Easter people involves a radical transformation of our identity. Here is an image that you might find helpful: When we consciously put our trust in Jesus, our old names go into God's obituary column. In that moment, God also places our new names in the divine birth column. God gives us a new identity. In the words of Paul, we have now been raised with Christ into a new life in God's kingdom. As the New Testament scholar Tom Wright puts it, "You were raised with the Messiah; so you possess a true life in God's new world, the 'upper' or 'heavenly' world. That's where the real 'you' is now to be found."*

In case this all sounds super-spiritual, let me describe one of the first down-to-earth consequences of our new identity. According to Paul, it relates to where we set our minds. As those who have been raised with Christ, we now set our minds on God's kingdom, on God's values, on God's dream for our world. We begin learning to think differently about our lives and choices. No longer do we pattern our thinking on how people in the world around us think, nor do we obey blindly what we are told to do. Rather, we focus our thinking on things above. The most important change that comes with our new identity in Christ is the transformation of our minds.

*Tom Wright, *New Testament Wisdom for Everyone*, (London: SPCK, 2013).

What does this mean in practical terms? To begin with, we know that what counts most, according to the thinking of the world, is to be successful, powerful, and rich. But people whose identity is shaped by their belonging to Christ think differently. What ultimately counts most in the kingdom of God is not success but faithfulness, not power but servanthood, not material riches but being rich in the Spirit. While this change in our thinking does not automatically lead to a change in behavior, it does point our lives in a new direction. How wonderful it will be if overnight we are transformed from self-centered, selfish, and greedy people into people whose minds and lives are centered only on God and God's dream for the world.

As Easter people, we affirm our new identity: We have been raised with Christ. Now, with the help of his Spirit, let us learn to think and live differently.

### *Daily Practice*

Choose today, in whatever situation you find yourself, to consciously set your mind on what you believe the Spirit wants to happen.

# DEATH

*Put to death, therefore, whatever belongs*
*to your earthly nature:*
*sexual immorality, impurity, lust,*
*evil desires and greed, which is idolatry.*
**Colossians 3:5**

As Easter people we become newly created human beings. Wonderfully, as God places us in the divine birth column, we are given a new identity. We are now people who have been raised with Christ. Today's word reminds us what this means for us. Not only does it mean that we must think differently but we are also challenged to live differently. Living in God's new world involves setting our minds on those things above, as we saw yesterday, and then working out what this practically means in our everyday behavior.

In the verse above, Paul's language becomes startlingly stern. He tells us to put to death ways of behaving and desiring and speaking that sabotage our new identity. This is something that we must do. God will not do it for us. We must ensure that those things holding us back from living our new lives in Christ are put to death. Paul's specific list of what we need to kill off includes sexual misbehavior, selfishness, idolizing money, destructive patterns of speech, telling lies, and so on. (See Colossians 3:1-17.)

How do we go about doing this? As a learner in these matters, I begin by reminding myself of my new identity. I am someone loved, forgiven, and accepted by God. I have been raised with Christ. With Paul's list as a guide, I ask the Spirit to reveal what in me needs to die for me to experience my risen life. Whatever it may be—lying, pride, or greediness—I also find it helpful to trace the history of this particular sinful pattern in my life over the years. How has it affected the lives of those around me? How has it blocked my own growth in faith? Asking for the help of God's grace, I resolve to let go of it and to replace it with a more faithful expression of my new identity. Often this will involve putting into practice a helpful and relevant spiritual discipline.

Perhaps you are thinking that this sounds like too much hard work. Not at all when we consider what is at stake here. Learning to die to our old selves is a lifelong journey that leads us toward putting on new selves that reflect the image of Christ. What could be better?

## *Daily Practice*

Take time to read slowly through the list of those things that Paul wants you to put to death. You will find it in Colossians 3:1-17. What do you need to deal with? Speak with God about it today.

# PUT ON

*Do not lie to each other, since you have taken off your old self*
*with its practices and have put on the new self,*
*which is being renewed in knowledge*
*in the image of its Creator.*
**Colossians 3:9-10**

Putting on our clothes for the day is an early morning ritual we all take part in. Usually there are a few factors that we take into account as we do this. *What is the weather forecast for the day? Will it be hot, cold, or mild? Will the sun shine, or will it rain? What are the tasks I need to do during the day? Will I be going to work, relaxing at home, working in the garden, entertaining friends, or meeting important people?* Usually the choice of what clothes to wear boils down to one main thing: *Will I be dressed suitably or not?*

Easter people put on a particular set of clothes each day. These clothes suit our new identity as Easter people. As people who have been raised with Christ, we are now part of the new creation that God is bringing about. Not only are there certain practices that we must get rid of, but also we are called to clothe ourselves in such a way that we reflect more visibly the image of our Creator. Again, this is not something that God will do for us. While the Holy Spirit will certainly help us, we will need to be intentional. After all, one critical step in our growing up is that transitional moment when we take responsibility for dressing ourselves.

Read again carefully Colossians 3:9-10. Take a long look at the clothes hanging up in God's closet waiting for you to put on.

Inspect each item of clothing, one by one. There is compassion, kindness, humility, gentleness, patience, forgiveness, and, above all, love, which binds them all together. Think for a moment how these virtues are reflected in the gospel life of Jesus himself. Ask yourself what sort of actions and words would make these virtues more real in your life at home, in your workplace, and within your community.

Putting on our new clothes as Easter people does not happen quickly or easily. It involves daily decision, determination, discarding practices of the old self that are not okay, and getting suitably dressed every morning. It takes a lifetime, but, as Walter Burghardt, SJ has written, the risen Christ now living in us makes possible a risen life, a human life above the human.*

## *Daily Practice*

The next time you get dressed for the day, consciously put on one item of clothing from God's closet. Ask for the help of the Holy Spirit in making this particular virtue more visible in your life. When you get undressed, reflect on how it went throughout the day.

*Walter J. Burghardt, SJ, *The Image of God in Man According to Cyril of Alexandria* (Eugene, OR: WiPf and Stock Publishers, 1957), 37.

*Day 16*

# HOVERING

*Now the earth was formless and empty,*
*darkness was over the surface of the deep,*
*and the Spirit of God was hovering over the waters.*
**Genesis 1:2**

The first image given to us in the Bible is beautifully poignant and powerful. It is the picture of God's Spirit hovering over the primal chaos. Because of the presence of the Holy Spirit, we know that chaos is not going to have the final word. There is the always present possibility that God will bring beauty, meaning, and order into the murky mess. As we read further in the first chapter of Genesis, this is certainly what happens. The Spirit causes chaos to become cosmos.

We are no strangers to chaos. Sometimes the chaos is internal as we wrestle with conflicting desires and yearnings, tearing us in different directions. Or sometimes we struggle to hold our close relationships together in the midst of the demands of everyday life. Chaos threatens as we seek to earn an income in a tough work environment or as we wrestle with an addiction sabotaging our lives. Or we might battle a potentially life-threatening illness or live in a community torn apart by violence and crime. For some of us, chaos almost becomes the new normal.

The good news is that the Spirit of God hovers over our chaos. Just as in the first Creation story, there is always the potential for the Spirit to bring beauty out of the ugliness, meaning out of the mess, and order out of the unformed. The important task for us is to stay aware and responsive to the creative actions of the Spirit hovering over our lives. We need to ask, *What are the new, unexplored possibilities emerging in our lives, our relation-ships, our work, and our community? How can we cooperate with these life-giving opportunities?*

Easter people constantly ask the Holy Spirit to hover over their chaos and to bring about new creation. Will you ask this of the Holy Spirit today?

### *Daily Practice*

Name your chaos before God today. Ask for the Holy Spirit to hover over you. Look for the signs of new creation breaking out within and around you.

# CRAFT

*Moses said to the Israelites,*
*"See, the Lord has chosen Bezalel son of Uri,*
*the son of Hur, of the tribe of Judah,*
*and he has filled him with the Spirit of God,*
*with wisdom, with understanding,*
*with knowledge and with all kinds of skills—*
*to make artistic designs for work in gold,*
*silver and bronze, to cut and set stones, to work in wood*
*and to engage in all kinds of artistic crafts.*
**Exodus 35:30-33**

Have you noticed how often we "spiritualize" the work of the Holy Spirit? More often than not, when we speak about the Holy Spirit, we tend to confine the activity of God's Spirit to what we do at church. We talk about the Spirit moving in a time of worship, speaking to us through the sermon, or giving us words when we pray with someone in need. These are the activities that come to mind when we think about being inspired, or filled, by the Holy Spirit. While these are certainly important aspects of the work of the Holy Spirit, we dare not limit the inspiration of the Spirit to churchy moments.

Carefully read again the Bible verse for today. Notice the kinds of activities in which the Holy Spirit is involved. The Holy Spirit is helping artists and craftsperson to work with greater competence and effectiveness. What wonderful good news this is for us today! As we go about our labor, the inspiration of the Holy Spirit wants to mingle with the perspiration of our efforts, whatever our own particular craft or activity may be. The Spirit of God also wants to fill us with skill, ability, and knowledge so that we may also be more competent and effective in our work. The work of the Holy Spirit in our lives goes far beyond Sunday worship. It extends into whatever we give our energy and effort to throughout the week.

I wonder what your work looks like each day. Whatever it is—teaching at a school, running a business, working in a factory, nursing in a hospital, typing on a computer, caring for grandchildren, making meals for the family, looking after a small garden, selling your company's product, managing an engineering or building project, playing a professional sport, fixing electrical or plumbing problems the Holy Spirit wants to help you to do whatever you do a little bit better. Our daily work becomes our worship, and our worship becomes our daily work. Our lives, through the whole week, bring greater glory to God.

### *Daily Practice*

As you engage in your daily craft, ask the Holy Spirit to combine with your skill, ability, and knowledge so that you may work better.

# WHERE

*Where can I go from your Spirit?*
*Where can I flee from your presence?*
**Psalm 139:7**

Many of us live with a split spirituality. This happens whenever we divide our lives into what we call *sacred* and *secular* compartments. On the one hand, we have the religious compartment of our lives. This part consists of when we pray, go to church, study the Bible, attend a retreat, and so on. On the other hand, there is the nonreligious compartment of our lives. This is the part that involves things like going to work, hanging out with friends, playing a sport, shopping at the mall, and going on vacation. We tend to connect the Holy Spirit with the first part and not the second.

The psalmist encourages us to see our lives differently. We are never away from the presence of God's Spirit. The Holy Spirit is present and active in every encounter at home, in our daily work, in our communities, and, indeed, throughout the whole universe. We experience the Holy Spirit all the time. The Spirit of God is always reaching out to us with God's love and grace in moments of beauty, rest, intimacy, joy, and newness. Even in times of heartache and heartbreak, the Holy Spirit seeks to touch us with comfort, consolation, and concern. Wherever we are, God's Spirit is present and active.

This is where the spiritual practice of "noticing" comes in. While God is most certainly present and active in every experience, encounter, and event of our lives, we can so easily fail to recognize and respond to this ever-present activity of the

Divine Spirit. We need to learn to "notice" the movements of the Spirit within and around us. We should never split our spirituality into two compartments. The Holy Spirit is present in every breath we take, every task we do, every bite of food we eat, every hug we receive, and every person we meet, always seeking to bring us more alive to the mystery of God in every part of our existence.

Easter people know that religion is not their lives. Their lives are their religion. They know that where they are, God is always present and active.

### Daily Practice

Reflect on the past hour. Where and how has God's Spirit been present and active? Give thanks to God.

# ABBA

*The Spirit you received does not make you slaves,*
*so that you live in fear again;*
*rather, the Spirit you received*
*brought about your adoption to sonship.*
*And by him we cry, "Abba, Father."*
**Romans 8:15**

One of the deepest things that the Holy Spirit does within us is to help us to cry out "Abba" when we come to God. It is one thing to acknowledge God formally as our heavenly Parent when we say the Lord's Prayer. It is quite another matter to interact with God intimately and personally when we pray. Our hearts yearn for this. When we come to God, we long to know, deep down in our hearts and minds, that we are coming to someone who really loves us, who knows us personally by name, and who has our good at heart. When we don't know this, we can so easily go through life feeling like orphans in the universe.

*Abba* was the word that Jesus used when he spoke with God. When Jesus addressed God in this way, it would have surprised those around him. It was not the usual formal way in which the Jewish religious leaders spoke to God in their prayers and worship. It was a tender, intimate, affectionate word. Jewish children would use it as they ran toward their fathers. In today's Bible verse, Paul tells us that the same Spirit who moved Jesus to cry, "Abba," now lives in us and helps us to share in the same kind of familial relationship that Jesus has with God. We too are prompted to cry out as Jesus did, "Abba, Father."

Rather than experiencing ourselves as lonely orphans, we know now that we belong as adopted children in God's family.

This "Abba experience" is not something that we can manufacture, achieve, or produce through our own efforts. Nor does it depend on any special learning, ability, or skill. It is an inner knowing, an inward assurance, given to us by God's Spirit. What matters most is that we remain open to the Holy Spirit who wants to make this experience possible for each one of us. Even when we don't know what to pray for or how to pray, we can know God in this intimate, tender, and affectionate way. This is the witness of Easter people throughout the ages. The Holy Spirit leads us into the mystery of the Trinity, whereby with Jesus, we cry out to God, "Abba, Father."

### *Daily Practice*

Take five minutes to be alone with God. Open yourself to the Holy Spirit and ask for a deeper "Abba experience." Consider repeating quietly the phrase: *Abba, I belong to you.*

# INTERCEDES

*The Spirit helps us in our weakness.*
*We do not know what we ought to pray for,*
*but the Spirit himself*
*intercedes for us through wordless groans.*
**Romans 8:26**

Sometimes in our praying we come to the end of words. We don't have the words to express what we want. Here is one common example: For some time we have prayed for someone's healing or maybe for our own. We pray continuously, but nothing positive seems to happen. Things remain the same, or they even get worse. We begin to ask questions: *Is it because we are praying the wrong way? Or have we failed to discern rightly what we need to pray for? Or is it because we have lacked faith, not prayed enough, or lacked expectation in our praying?* I am sure you have experienced a dilemma like this at some stage in your praying, if not in your prayers for healing, then for some other situation.

It is encouraging to know that Paul identifies with us in our struggle to pray. He does not say, "You do not know what you ought to pray for," but "We do not know what we ought to pray for." Strikingly, in response to the struggles we sometimes have with prayer, Paul does not give us a new method or tell us we need more faith. Instead, he encourages us with the good news that the Holy Spirit comes to our aid in these moments and intercedes for us with groans that words cannot express. The focus we need to have in our praying, as Anglican theologian

Tom Smail has pointed out, is not on something more that we have to do but on what God is doing within us on our behalf.*

There is a profound mystery in Paul's words. They suggest that there is a Spirit-breathed intercession taking place within us all the time. In our deepest parts, we are in an unceasing, constant, and never-ending connection with the living God. The treasure of prayer is hidden away in the soil of our lives. There is a prayer meeting going on in our hearts 24/7! Easter people know that they are always a prayed-in people. When we are struggling to know how or what to pray for, this is exactly when the Holy Spirit helps us the most. That's what I call really good news.

### *Daily Practice*

Here is an affirmation for the day. As often as you are able, affirm this truth for yourself: *Because the Holy Spirit is within me, I am a prayed-in person.*

*Tom Smail, *The Giving Gift: The Holy Spirit in Person* (London: Hodder and Stoughton, 1988), 201–214.

# FELLOWSHIP

*May the grace of the Lord Jesus Christ,*
*and the love of God,*
*and the fellowship of the Holy Spirit*
*be with you all.*
**2 Corinthians 13:14**

Imagine yourself in Paul's place as he finishes this letter to the Corinthians. He wants to offer a blessing from the Trinity in such a way that each Person's main characteristic gets emphasized. He thinks of Jesus Christ, and *grace* immediately comes into his mind. When he meditates on the Father, his thoughts focus on *love*. Now what word will he choose to say about the Holy Spirit? Will it be *power*? Or maybe *gifts*? He decides against it. He chooses the word *fellowship*. For Paul, this is the most important characteristic describing the Holy Spirit. The Holy Spirit constantly seeks to draw us into fellowship with the Father and the Son and with one another.

Because *fellowship* has become such a vague and weak word today, I was disappointed when I first read this passage. However, over time I have come to see the critical importance of Paul's choice of words. *Fellowship*, especially in its Greek translation, has a powerful meaning. It speaks of an intimate sharing of ourselves with one another and with God at all levels of our lives, ranging from the spiritual to the material. Think of Luke's description of the early church community inundated by the Holy Spirit: "All the believers were together and had everything in common. They sold property and possessions to give to anyone who had need. Every day they continued to meet together in the temple courts. They broke bread in their homes and ate together with glad and sincere hearts" (Acts 2:44-46).

The Holy Spirit is the Spirit of loving relationship, genuine friendship, and intimate connection. Right now, the Holy Spirit is active in us and is seeking to open us up to the Father and the Son and to one another. How are we going to respond? Are we going to reflect the individualistic tone of our society and resist the Spirit by continuing to live self-interested and self-focused lives? Or are we going to respond to the Spirit and allow ourselves to be drawn into the fellowship that the Spirit creates and gives us? We can be sure that if we choose the latter, it will involve taking very practical steps like praying and worshiping together, giving hospitality to strangers, enjoying meals with others, giving material resources to those struggling, and generally learning how to live a deeper, shared life.

Spirit-filled Easter people are known much more by the quality of their relationships with one another than by any powerful gift they may exercise. Certainly, this is what Paul makes clear.

### *Daily Practice*
Do something practical today that expresses your belonging to others in the fellowship of the Holy Spirit.

Day 22

# COUNSELOR

*"I will ask the Father,
and he will give you another advocate
to help you and be with you forever. . . ."*
**John 14:16**

There are moments when we need consolation. Someone misunderstands us and makes an unfair judgment about us. A dear friend betrays us with false accusations behind our back. We are excluded from our church for some reason. A terrible depression descends bringing a sense of disconnection from everything and everyone around us. We lose someone whom we have loved deeply. In painful moments like these, and there are countless others like them, we need to know someone has our back and is there for us. We need to know that we are not alone. We need someone who will be with us through it all.

As Christ followers, we celebrate the good news that the Paraclete lives in us and consoles us. The *Paraclete* is my favorite title for the Holy Spirit. Gospel writer John uses the word four times in chapters 14 to 16, including in the verse above where it is interpreted *Counselor* or *Advocate*. It carries many rich meanings that are difficult to translate into one English word. Primarily it speaks of someone who counsels us, defends us, speaks on our behalf, comes to our aid, and comforts us. I love these words of Jean Vanier: "The Paraclete is given to those who are lonely and need the presence of a friend, to those who are lost and poor in spirit and who cry out to God."* In a way that goes far beyond words, the Holy Spirit consoles us as Jesus consoled his disciples.

But we need to take this one step further. As Easter people, we are empowered to become paracletes to others in need. God calls us to give the same consolation to those in need that we have received ourselves. Through our lips, hands, and eyes, we must allow the consolation of Jesus to flow toward those around us. We need to embody the spirit of consolation. In the words of Saint Francis's well-known prayer, "Let us not so much seek to be consoled, as to console, to be understood, as to understand." This is what the Holy Spirit comes to do in and through us. We are given the strength and the energy to witness to the consolation and comfort of God to a desperate and hurting world.

Right now, open yourself to the breath of the Paraclete breathing into you the consolation that only Jesus can give. Know that there is Someone who has your back and who is there for you. Know that you are not alone.

### *Daily Practice*

Take some time to say the words the prayer of Saint Francis, above. Think of one person in need with whom you can spend a few moments today.

*Jean Vanier, *Dawn into the Mystery of Jesus through the Gospel of John* (New York: Paulist Press, 2004), 260.

# REMIND

*"The Advocate, the Holy Spirit,*
*whom the Father will send in my name,*
*will teach you all things*
*and will remind you of everything I have said to you."*
**John 14:26**

One of our most prevalent sins is that of forgetfulness. We suffer from large doses of spiritual amnesia. We forget who God is. We forget who we are. We forget who we are called to be. We forget who our sister or brother is. The effects of this forgetfulness reverberate throughout our lives. Called to worship God, we worship things. Called to be sons and daughters of God, we live as orphans. Called to be mature, we remain children. Called to love, we remain self-centered. Tragically, we miss the mark God has set for our lives here on earth.

In this regard, our verse today emphasizes another important dimension of the Holy Spirit's activity: reminding us of everything we have learned from Jesus. Here is our antidote to our loss of spiritual memory. As we remain open to the Spirit, the Spirit helps us remember what Jesus has taught us. The Gospels—the sayings and stories of Jesus—are a great treasure. The Holy Spirit reminds us of these riches and constantly reveals their personal meanings in our lives. We could say that the Spirit personalizes the word of Christ for us just when we need it. An external gospel word becomes an internal experience of the risen Christ speaking to us in a personal way.

You may know what I am trying to describe from your own experience. The Spirit personalizes the gospel when we face difficult situations, when we don't know what to say, or when we are uncertain about the way ahead. Suddenly, something that Jesus has said in the Gospels comes alive for us with remarkable clarity and power, bringing us both consolation and challenge. We sense that we are being reminded of what we already know. We realize that the Spirit is helping us to comprehend more fully who God is, who we are, who we are called to be, and who our neighbor is. This is the Paraclete present and active in our lives!

### *Daily Practice*

Ask the Holy Spirit to remind you of one thing that Jesus teaches in the Gospels. Share this word with one other person.

# TESTIFY

*"When the Advocate comes,*
*whom I will send to you from the Father—*
*the Spirit of truth who goes out from the Father—*
*he will testify about me."*
**John 15:26**

One moment from my own early faith story stands out in my memory. I had just made my first public commitment to Jesus at a youth rally. Afterward, I sat with one of the counselors, who prayed with me. He then gave me my first bit of spiritual advice. He said, "Make sure you tell someone soon about the step you have taken tonight." When I asked him why I needed to do this, he answered, "If you don't share what you have been given, you will lose what you have received." In the language of the verse above, my counselor was encouraging me to testify to my experience of Jesus Christ. When we have experienced a spiritual awakening or renewal, we need to pass on what we have received because, when we do this, it helps our faith to grow and deepen. If we don't, it shrivels up and dies. Testifying to Christ not only brings blessings to those around us but it also blesses us. However, we need to be aware that those who hear our story may resent us if we talk about our faith in an unhelpful way. Rather than give Jesus a good reputation, pushy, judgmental, and self-righteous, words can turn people off. We always need God's help to give genuine testimony to our faith.

Again, Easter people know that this is another way in which the Holy Spirit helps us. Sometimes the Spirit helps us know when to listen and when to speak. On other occasions, the Spirit may create just the right opportunity for us to share our faith. Someone may ask us why we live the way we do, may share a real need with us, or may ask us a question about God. These moments can become little openings for us to share how we have experienced Christ in the struggle and crises of our lives. And as we share our faith, often struggling to find the right words, the Holy Spirit uses them to communicate Christ in a real and surprising way.

Every day we are surrounded by people who desperately need Jesus Christ. Are we willing to become involved in the challenging task of testifying about our faith? The Holy Spirit is ready to help us.

### *Daily Practice*

What have you come to know about Jesus Christ in your experience? Write one paragraph to clarify your thoughts and feelings.

# TRUTH

*"When he, the Spirit of truth, comes,*
*he will guide you into all the truth.*
*He will not speak on his own;*
*he will speak only what he hears,*
*and he will tell you what is yet to come."*
**John 16:13**

We hear much today about fake news. As we watch the news on TV, read the newspapers, or catch up on the headlines on our mobile phones, we are never too sure if what we are hearing or seeing is true. However, this uncertainty about what is true extends far beyond the daily news. Think about some of the big questions we ask: *Who is God? Who am I? How does God want me to live?* There are plenty of answers circulating out there on the street. Which ones are untrue? Which can we trust? Deciding what is true with regard to these questions completely determines the ultimate shape of our lives.

As our Paraclete, the Holy Spirit comes to guide us into all the truth. Jesus himself says to his followers, "I am the way and the truth and the life" (John 14:6). As the unique Son of the Father, he reveals the truth about what God is really like, the truth about who we are, and the truth about how God wants us to live. Some people of his day were drawn to this truth found in Jesus while many others resisted it and wanted to do away with him. Still today, announcing that the truth can be found in a person arouses powerful questions. After all, is it not the height of arrogance to suggest that the truth can only be found in one person?

Whatever your response to this astonishing claim made by Jesus, will you allow the Holy Spirit to be your guide? If yes, how? My suggestion is that you ask the Spirit some specific requests. Let me mention a few that you can address to the Holy Spirit. You can start praying: *Please reveal to me the truth of who God is. Show me how much I am worth to my Creator. How do you want me to live?* You can be sure that God's Spirit will take your prayer seriously. Together, with countless others throughout history, you will discover over time and through your own experience that the Holy Spirit indeed does lead us into all truth.

### *Daily Practice*

Pray to the Holy Spirit the suggested words above as you go through your daily life. As you pray, make a serious commitment to God, stating that you desire to know what is true.

# ANOINTED

*"The Spirit of the Lord is upon me*
*because he has anointed me*
*to proclaim good news to the poor."*
**Luke 4:18**

Anointing has a rich history in the Bible. In the Old Testament, kings and priests were anointed with perfumed oil. Significantly, when Jesus refers to being anointed by the Spirit of the Lord for ministry, there is no mention of oil. He is anointed directly by the Spirit of God. Why does he speak of being anointed, which suggests fragrant oil, if no ointment is used? The answer is obvious. When Jesus is anointed, the Holy Spirit is the oil. What the oil did for the kings and priests who were anointed in the Old Testament, the Holy Spirit does for Jesus. Not surprisingly, oil has come to symbolize the Holy Spirit in Christian ceremonies.

As Easter people, we need to be anointed with the "oil" of the Spirit. Being spiritually anointed suggests a distinctive fragrance that communicates the presence of Jesus alive in us. It may be expressed through the aroma of an overwhelming generosity toward those in need, through a peaceful serenity and unusual calmness in the midst of trouble, or in a simple authority and inward power about the way we teach and preach. In whatever way our lives may smell of this sweet scent, we begin to smell like genuine followers of Jesus when God's Spirit anoints us.

What do we smell like? As his disciples, we already have been anointed by Christ himself. (See 1 John 2: 20.) The oil of the Spirit is, to use a Gospel image, bottled up in the alabaster jars of our lives. Catholic theologian and writer Raniero Cantalamessa suggests that these jars need to be broken so that the fragrance of the Spirit can be set free in our lives.* Each of us needs to think about what this may mean. Often, this breaking involves vulnerably opening ourselves to God, abandoning ourselves to Jesus, and dying to our self-contentedness. Whatever efforts we need to make, they always must be accompanied by a simple request for the Lord to anoint us with his Spirit whenever we intend to do something for him. Only then will we become the aroma of Christ!

### *Daily Practice*

Today, whenever you begin a new task that you want to do on behalf of the Lord, ask God to anoint you with the oil of the Holy Spirit.

*Raniero Cantalamessa, *Life in Christ: A Spiritual Commentary on the Letter to the Romans* (Collegeville, MN: Liturgical Press, 1997).

# LOVE

*Hope does not put us to shame,*
*because God's love has been poured out into our hearts*
*through the Holy Spirit, who has been given to us.*
**Romans 5:5**

There is an immense difference between knowing something with our heads and knowing something with our hearts. This is especially true when it comes to the different truths of our faith. For example, it is one thing to affirm intellectually that God is love, but it is a totally different thing to know inside ourselves that God loves us personally with a love that will never let us go. For many of us, the longest journey in our faith walk is for our doctrine to travel from our heads to our hearts. When that happens, we begin to know God in firsthand, vital, and transforming ways.

In today's verse, Paul reminds us that God pours God's love into our hearts through the gift of the Holy Spirit. How does this happen for you and me? In God's kingdom, divine love operates in two ways. It must be both received and given. We cannot give the love of God to others if we have not first received it. Receiving is always the first movement in our relationship with God. Then, we share God's love with others. If God's love does not flow through us to others, then we block the Spirit's ability to pour God's love into our hearts on an ongoing basis. To what extent is this two-way movement of God's love at work in your life today?

Perhaps this idea of God's personal love is somewhat abstract for you. Remind yourself that the Holy Spirit is the deeply personal love of God in the here and now. Right where you are, ask the Holy Spirit to help you experience the warmth of your heavenly Parent's love in your heart. Is there a blockage in your heart caused by a refusal to love someone you know? Set your will deliberately toward loving that person with the love of God. Ask God to help you to do this and to discern how best to express the divine love in a particular situation. As you do this, your heart will start to beat again with a renewed sense of God's love. May the journey from your head to your heart begin!

### *Daily Practice*

Find a quiet space. Picture the faces of those who love you. Allow yourself to feel their love. Remind yourself that God loves you at least as much as the person who loves you most. Put your hand on your heart and ask the Holy Spirit to help you feel the love of God.

# BODY

*Do you not know that your bodies*
*are temples of the Holy Spirit,*
*who is in you, whom you have received from God?*
**1 Corinthians 6:19**

How do you feel about your body? Quite rarely do we meet persons who are totally comfortable with their bodies. Provocative images that remind us we live in a culture that worships a youthful body and physical attractiveness bombard us each day. Not surprisingly, we struggle with any sign of bodily decay that reminds us we are getting older. We may even end up living in fear of our bodies and what they may do to us. Sadly, there is sometimes a tendency in Christian circles to view the body as an enemy of the spiritual life. What are your thoughts regarding the role of your body in your journey with God?

Today the apostle Paul invites us to view our bodies from a different perspective. He asks us to see them as temples of the Holy Spirit. In Jewish thought the Temple represents that sacred place where heaven and earth come together, where the Holy One is present, and where we offer ourselves to God. This is the image Paul asks his friends in the Corinthian church to consider when thinking about their bodies. We can be reasonably sure that they had difficulty imagining their bodies in this light. If we are honest with ourselves, we don't do much better. Few of us live with the constant awareness that we should treasure our bodies as the places where God wants to take up residence.

But we can learn to think differently about our present bodies. There are a number of stepping stones in this learning process. Dallas Willard suggests we begin by surrendering our bodies to God. What we want is that God should fill our bodies even more fully with the divine Presence. Next, we can consider how we abuse our bodies, especially through overwork and substance abuse, and take steps toward practicing sabbath rest. Getting enough sleep is a good start. Lastly, because God's Spirit inhabits our bodies, we can honor God with them as we regularly dedicate each part to God's service where we are. Easter people know that their bodies are temples of the Holy Spirit!

### *Daily Practice*

Spend some time expressing care for your body. Whatever you may do, whether it is taking a leisurely bath, lying down to rest, or going for a walk around the block, give thanks to God that your body is a temple of God's Spirit.

# DESERT

*Jesus was led by the Spirit*
*into the wilderness*
*to be tempted by the devil.*
**Matthew 4:1**

Have you noticed that everything we are able to do competently in this life requires hidden preparation? Think of the pianist playing a piece of music beautifully, the surgeon successfully performing a delicate operation, the athlete breaking a long-standing record, the speaker delivering an inspiring talk, the teacher giving an outstanding lesson, or the plumber effectively fixing a blocked drain. All these people, in order to do their tasks well, have put in many hours of practice and learning that no one sees. Living life well on-the-spot always requires off-the-spot preparation.

We see the Holy Spirit involved in this same dynamic in the story of Jesus' life. Before the curtains open on Jesus' messianic ministry, the Spirit leads him into the desert. There Jesus wrestles with and overcomes three crucial temptations with regard to the shape of his public ministry. No one witnesses these behind-the-scenes moments in his life. They take place completely out of the public eye. His on-the-spot ministry with others is backed by this off-the-spot engagement with God in the solitude of the desert.

Is the Holy Spirit leading you into the "desert"? How is the Spirit working to better prepare you for your everyday walk with Jesus? It is highly unlikely that your desert experience will involve forty days in an actual geographical desert. But it may be a day alone at a nearby retreat center, a time of personal Bible study on your own, or a weekend away in the mountains. Whatever shape your desert-solitude takes, you can be sure that the Holy Spirit will be present, preparing your heart and mind for a more powerful witness in the public sphere. This is what Easter people throughout the ages have come to know. The desert is the training ground of the Holy Spirit for those who want to be faithful, effective, and competent in the rest of their lives.

### *Daily Practice*

Carve out a desert moment of solitude today. Allow it to be a time when you can simply be alone with God and yourself. It doesn't need to be long; between ten and fifteen minutes will be enough.

# TRANSFORMED

*We all, who with unveiled faces reflect the Lord's glory,*
*are being transformed into his image with ever-increasing glory,*
*which comes from the Lord, who is the Spirit.*
**2 Corinthians 3:18**

As people of faith, we constantly face the challenge of being credible to the people around us. In fact, it could be the greatest challenge facing us at the present moment of history. Are we living signs of contradiction to the world's dominant values centered around money, sex, and power? Do our faces reflect the radiant presence of Christ with ever-increasing glory? Is there any evidence that the Holy Spirit is transforming our self-centered lives into a greater likeness of Christ? As an atheist once said to those Christians he knew, "I will believe in your Savior when you look more saved."

Constantly, we need to remind ourselves that the Holy Spirit is the great Transformer. We cannot just stay the same. From the inside out, the Lord who is Spirit wants to change us into "little Christs." It is an inward change that goes far beyond the external. It is a total renovation of our lives on the inside— the renovation of our hearts, our will, our thoughts, and our feelings—that involves a process of transformation that causes us to reflect the glory of Jesus wherever we are. Ultimately, only this kind of transformed life will serve as an adequate response to the credibility challenge.

How does this inner change take place? On the one hand, we must grasp that it is the work of the Holy Spirit who changes us. It is not something that we bring about ourselves by trying harder to be like Jesus. It is always an inner work of the Spirit, a gift of grace given to us as we live with open hands before God. On the other hand, we need to cooperate with the Spirit. Inner change does not fall from heaven on the lazy and the passive. We need to work with the Spirit to become the people God wants us to be. This is one reason each meditation in *Pauses for Pentecost* comes with a simple daily practice. The daily practices are there to open our lives more widely to the transforming grace of the Spirit. After all, "faith by itself, if it is not accompanied by action, is dead" (James 2:17).

### *Daily Practice*

Take five to ten minutes to sit with open hands before God. Pray simply, *Holy Spirit, make me like Jesus.* Repeat this prayer whenever you need to today.

# DEVOUT

*There was a man in Jerusalem called Simeon,*
*who was righteous and devout.*
*He was waiting for the consolation of Israel,*
*and the Holy Spirit was on him.*
**Luke 2:25**

Easter people believe that we live each day in the overlapping of two realities. On the one hand, there is our earthly space in which we go about our daily activities. This is the visible realm that we get to know through our five senses. On the other hand, there is the heavenly space where God lives and reigns. This is the invisible realm that we discover when we start trusting and following Christ. The big question for us is: *How do we discern how and where God is at work around us?*

Simeon was a Spirit-filled person who learned to do this. He was old and had patiently waited to see God's saving work in his lifetime. When Jesus' parents took Jesus as a child to the Temple courts, Simeon immediately recognized that this was a God moment. He took Jesus in his arms, praised God, and cried out, "Sovereign Lord, as you have promised, you can now dismiss your servant in peace. For my eyes have seen your salvation, which you have prepared in the sight of all nations, a light of revelation to the Gentiles, and for glory to your people Israel" (Luke 2:29-32).

What was the source of his deep spiritual sensitivity? Put bluntly, Simeon is devout. Three times in two verses his name is associated with the Holy Spirit. Obviously, he lives a God-yielded, God-filled, God-committed life. His passionate devotion finds special expression in his study of the scriptures. All the words he speaks come from the prophetic vision of Isaiah in chapters 40–55. Simeon recognizes what God is doing because he is open to God and regular in devotion. He devotes himself to God and to a prayerful study of scripture. Are we willing to follow his example?

### *Daily Practice*

Think of one way you deliberately can express your devotion to God today. With the help of God's Spirit, express that devotion over the next few hours.

# DWELL

*I pray that out of his glorious riches*
*he may strengthen you with power*
*through his Spirit in your inner being,*
*so that Christ may dwell*
*in your hearts through faith.*
**Ephesians 3:16-17**

Popular Christian vocabulary often uses the phrase "Invite Jesus into your heart. The danger of language like this is that it easily can encourage a private and sentimental understanding of our faith. However, there is also something beautiful and important about this image. You and I can become his dwelling place in the here and now. Our faith teaches that Jesus once lived long ago, taught and did miracles, died and rose again. More importantly, faith means that he lives in us and works through us today to bless the lives of others.

All this happens through the power of God's Spirit. Through the Holy Spirit we come to know Jesus personally. Rather than giving us theoretical knowledge about Christ, the Holy Spirit takes what we have heard and read about Jesus and makes these things real for us. Doctrines about Jesus Christ are important, but more importantly we need to experience that he is alive and that he can work in the world through our lives. The Holy Spirit makes this firsthand knowledge of Christ possible for us. Through the indwelling Spirit, Jesus makes his home in us. Quite literally, we must become the place where Christ dwells in the present.

Perhaps today you can ask the Holy Spirit to help you hear Jesus saying these words to you: *I want to come and dwell in your life. Through you I want to touch the lives of those around you. Be willing to let go of your own agendas and plans that so often keep you from living and acting in and through me. Let yourself be led, strengthened, and renewed by my own Spirit living in your inner being. As you do, you "may have power, together with all the Lord's holy people, to grasp how wide and long and high and deep is the love of Christ, and to know this love that surpasses knowledge—that you may be filled to the measure of all the fullness of God"* (Eph. 3:18-19).

### *Daily Practice*

Find a quiet space where you can spend some time alone. In the silence, ask the Holy Spirit to help you hear Jesus' words above addressed to you. Place your hand on your heart and know that Christ dwells in you.

# GUIDE

*The LORD will guide you always;*
*he will satisfy your needs in a sun-scorched land*
*and will strengthen your frame.*
**Isaiah 58:11**

Each day we make decisions. Sometimes they are big ones involving careers, business options, significant relationships, and finances. Then we make smaller ones about how we need to spend our time, what we pay attention to now, or what we leave for another day. Every choice we make gets written into the texture of our lives forever. We become who we are through the decisions we make or don't make. So we ask questions: *How do we make decisions in tune with God's heart for us? How does the Lord guide us? How do we know that the Lord is guiding us?*

Generally speaking, we know what the Lord wants for our lives. We all know that God wants us to love, to be honest, to serve others, and to do as much good as we are able to do. However, we still need to know how best to do these things within our everyday encounters and events. Thankfully, we are not left to work this out alone. An important part of the work of the Holy Spirit is to guide us in the Lord's way as we make decisions each day. This has been the testimony of Easter people throughout the ages, from the early church described in the book of Acts to the present day.

Here is the invitation: Are we willing to entrust each day, with all its decisions, to the inner guidance of the Spirit in our lives? In our hectic lives we are prone to live on autopilot without any conscious consultation with the Holy Spirit. While the

Spirit is not going to give us a computer printout with exactly what to do in every decision we face, consulting the Spirit in prayer gives our divine Friend access to shine light on the next step we may need to take. More often than not, this inner guidance resembles Christlike thought, and a deep sense of God's peace accompanies it. As my spiritual director often says to me, "The Lord always leads us in peace."

### *Daily Practice*

Talk with the Lord about a decision you are presently facing. Think about your different options. On which option does the peace of the Lord rest most powerfully?

# RESPONSIBILITY

*"Brothers and sisters,*
*choose seven men from among you*
*who are known to be full of the Spirit and wisdom.*
*We will turn this responsibility over to them*
*and will give our attention to prayer*
*and the ministry of the word."*
**Acts 6:3-4**

I love the down-to-earth way the Holy Spirit wants to work in our lives. We often confine the work of the Holy Spirit to "spiritual" things, but the Spirit also wants to be involved in our immediate, everyday responsibilities. We see this in today's scripture reading. In the early church, a conflict developed between the Greek and Hebrew-speaking widows. The former claim that they have been neglected in the distribution of food. This is a mundane matter that needs to be resolved with integrity and fairness. In response, the apostles form a team of seven Spirit-filled men to do the work.

Are you as taken aback as I was when I first read this? Surely sorting out who sits at what table and distributing the food and meals are relatively straightforward tasks that anyone with common sense can do. But the apostles see more deeply. They understand that they will need all the resources and wisdom of the Spirit for this practical and everyday matter. One of the men chosen, Stephen, is described as a person "full of faith and of the Holy Spirit" (Acts 6:5). He goes on to become the first martyr in the early church.

During most of our days, we are involved in work and responsibilities that are unspectacular and not very glamorous. We do things like taking kids to school, making meals, creating spreadsheets, answering emails, sitting in business meetings, mending broken appliances, typing minutes of meetings, meeting with clients, preparing lessons—and the list of ordinary activities goes on and on. While we may not think so, these things need just as much integrity and wisdom as ministries done by more high-profile, spiritual leaders. Those who wait on tables need the Spirit just as much as those who preach, those who lead churches, and those who write Christian books! Are you surprised?

### *Daily Practice*

Today, see each of your daily responsibilities as an opportunity for you to live in the power of the Holy Spirit.

# ENCOURAGEMENT

*Joseph, a Levite from Cyprus,*
*whom the apostles called Barnabas*
*(which means "son of encouragement"). . . .*
**Acts 4:36**

Recently, I have noticed how many of our conversations are riddled with discouragement: discouragement about the political future of our country, about the work we do each day, about our closest relationships, and—most painfully—about our journey with God. Few things have more power to rob us of joy and happiness than being discouraged. This realization gets me thinking: As Easter people empowered by the Spirit, one of the most important ministries we are called to exercise today is the ministry of encouragement.

One of the unsung heroes of the early church is Barnabas. Joseph is his real name, but as the apostles watch him interact with people, they rename him *Barnabas*, which means "son of consolation" or "son of comfort." Elsewhere in the book of Acts, Luke describes him as "a good man, full of the Holy Spirit and faith," and by his witness "a great number of people were brought to the Lord" (Acts 11:24). As we entrust our lives to the Lord, his Spirit enables us to encourage people around us. Certainly this is the case with Barnabas. Hopefully, it can be true for us as well.

How did Barnabas exercise the ministry of encouragement? A quick glance at the times Luke mentions him in Acts gives us helpful clues. First, when he brings the newly converted Paul to the fearful and suspicious leadership of the church in Jerusalem, he acts as mediator. (See Acts 9:27.) Bridging gaps and bring-ing healing between conflicting parties can be a huge source of encouragement for those involved. Second, he constantly affirms followers of Christ who live faithfully and stand firm in their faith, and he expresses appreciation for them. (See Acts 11:23.) Third, he goes against Paul's advice and gives a young, impetuous John Mark a second chance. (See Acts 15:38-39.) Can you think of someone you can bless today through encour-agement and affirmation?

### *Daily Practice*

Seek to put into practice, both thoughtfully and intentionally, the ministry of encouragement wherever you are today.

# POWER

*My message and my preaching*
*were not with wise and persuasive words,*
*but with a demonstration of the Spirit's power,*
*so that your faith might not rest on human wisdom,*
*but on God's power.*
**1 Corinthians 2:4-5**

Most of us limp in one way or another. Our limp could be something physical, an addiction to some substance, an emotional wound from the past, a quirk of personality, or a problem in relationships. Whatever it is, our Achilles heel continually reminds us that we are not totally whole and healthy. But while it may cause us distress and despair, the good news is that our point of weakness is where God's Spirit wants to empower us and make us stronger.

Certainly, Paul the apostle would affirm this truth. He knows that God is a God of power. Twice in today's verse he refers to the power of God and God's Spirit. But he also knows that God's power will be shown in his weakness. We know by his own admission that he is not eloquent and captivating as a public speaker, yet he is convinced that God can work miracles in spite of his limp. Elsewhere he writes (concerning his struggle with his thorn in the flesh) that the Lord has said, "My grace is sufficient for you, for my power is made perfect in weakness" (2 Cor. 12:9).

How would you describe your own "limp," your own Achilles heel? We don't have to hide it, pretend that we have life all together, or allow our limp to disqualify us from God's work. It is precisely at our point of weakness that we can become spiritually strong. The crucial thing is to acknowledge our limp, share our struggle with our sisters and brothers in the faith, and trust God's grace to help us do what we cannot do in our own strength. Our lives can become, like Paul's life, an example of the Spirit's power. After all, this is what it means to live as Easter people empowered by the Holy Spirit.

### *Daily Practice*

Share your Achilles heel with the Lord and with one other person you trust. Ask God to help you anticipate the power of the Spirit where you limp.

# WATER

*"Whoever believes in me, as Scripture has said,*
*rivers of living water will flow from within them."*
**John 7:38**

Biblical writers repeatedly associate the Holy Spirit with water. This shouldn't surprise us. Living in arid areas often characterized by dryness and drought, they know from firsthand experience how they depend on the availability of water. Where there is water, there is always the possibility of fresh life. Water's absence means famine. As a result, in their search for symbols that will speak of the life-giving activity of God's Spirit, they naturally think of water. Water will come to symbolize the pouring out of the Holy Spirit, bringing life to a dry and thirsty land.

In Jesus' words above, he promises the gift of living water. Unlike water that stands and becomes stagnant, living water refers to receiving a certain kind of life from his Spirit, life which is continuous, always flowing, and never-ending. Jesus makes the bold claim that, through the gift of the Holy Spirit, he can satisfy our thirst forever. His "living water" will not fail us, let us down, or run dry. Jesus' living water is a stream of blessing that bubbles up from within us and flows through us to others. In the sometimes stifling and draining heat of daily life, this is surely one of our deepest needs.

We thirst in so many ways. We thirst for meaning and significance, for connection and intimacy, for affirmation and acceptance. When our thirst goes unquenched, we find ourselves dried up inside. Our lives become empty and barren and sick with unfulfilled longing. Our need for the living water that Jesus promises, the water of his presence and never-give-up love, is profound. Two simple verbs guide us in our response to Jesus' promise: *come* and *drink*. We come to Christ as we are in our need and in our longing. By faith we drink his refreshing, personal presence through his Spirit. In this constant pattern of coming and drinking, our desert-like lives blossom forth again with the life that God's Spirit gives.

### *Daily Practice*

With every glass of water you drink today, come to Christ and drink the living water he gives.

# DRUNK

*Do not get drunk on wine, which leads to debauchery.*
*Instead, be filled with the Spirit. . . .*
**Ephesians 5:18**

This verse suggests we can get drunk in two ways. We can get drunk with alcohol or with the Holy Spirit. Between these two options and their contrasts, consequences are massive. While both certainly can make us happy, the first way leaves us unsteady and uncertain on our feet, while the second way fills us with a new steadiness and confidence as we face the difficulties of life. When drunk with wine, we think unreasonably, we slur our words, our sight becomes blurred, and we end up with a hangover. When filled with the "new wine" of the Spirit, we think more deeply, communicate more effectively, see more clearly, and experience genuine happiness.

Think back to the Day of Pentecost in Acts 2. Have you ever thought about how, on the Day of Pentecost, Peter begins his sermon with these words: "Fellow Jews and all of you who live in Jerusalem, let me explain this to you; listen carefully to what I say. These people are not drunk, as you suppose. It's only nine in the morning!" (Acts 2:14-15). What is happening that Peter has to make this denial? Can it be that these Spirit-filled men and women are demonstrating what it is like to be drunk with the Spirit? Are they experiencing what some of the ancients have called "the sober intoxication of the Spirit"?

How do we journey toward this sober intoxication? On the one hand, we must always remember that this experience is a gift that God gives to us. It is God who fills us with God's Spirit.

We can receive this spiritual drink in moments of intense prayer, corporate worship, shared fellowship, or deep silence. On the other hand, we can actively prepare ourselves by becoming more sober in those areas of our lives where we run the danger of intoxication. What intoxicates us? It could be wine, drugs, success, money, applause, work, anxiety, or fear. As we acknowledge whatever intoxicates us and yield the reins of our lives to the risen Lord, we open ourselves to a greater experience of the Holy Spirit. We become Easter people filled with God's Spirit!

### *Daily Practice*

In what area of your life do you need to become more sober? Express your need to the Lord, and ask for the Holy Spirit to help you live more freely and fully today.

# LISTEN

*Whoever has ears,*
*let them hear what the Spirit says to the churches.*
**Revelation 3:6**

I wonder what you think God's biggest complaint in the Bible is. A few years ago, someone explained to me what it is. It may surprise you as it did me. It is not that God's people don't pray enough or fast enough or are not good enough. According to Klyne Snodgrass, after he had studied over 1,500 references to the words *listen* and *hear* in the Bible, God's biggest complaint is that people do not listen. If we do not obey God, it is proof that we have not really listened.

The God we worship is the God who constantly wants to communicate with us. This becomes clear in the second and third chapters of Revelation, where the above invitation becomes a constant refrain in the messages to the seven churches. Repeatedly, the people of God are told to listen to what the Spirit may be saying to them. While Spirit-inspired communication can happen in so many different and creative ways, the chief means of God's personal communication to us usually occurs within scripture. Nothing is more important for us than to hear what God may be saying to us through the pages of the Bible.

Listening to the Spirit speak to us in the Bible is something we learn. We are not inherently good at it. We find it easier to read the Bible to gain more knowledge rather than to hear God speaking to us. God invites each of us to develop our capacity to listen to the Spirit's whisper. We begin by reading a small portion of scripture carefully and unhurriedly. As we read, we wait for a word, a phrase, or a sentence to get our attention. This may be the Spirit speaking to us. When this happens, we take in what we are reading and think about it more deeply. Lastly, we talk with God about what it may mean for us to live out in our daily lives what we have heard. Listening and obedience always go together. We listen in order to discern how to live differently. Spirit-filled Easter people are people who seek to listen and obey!

### *Daily Practice*

Practice listening to the Spirit today. Take your favorite passage of scripture and read it, following the simple steps outlined in the previous paragraph.

# WITHDREW

*While [Jesus] was blessing them,*
*he left them and was taken up into heaven.*
**Luke 24:51**

Goodbyes are painful. They happen in so many different ways. Someone we love immigrates to a country across the ocean, gets transferred to work in another city, or leaves for college far away. Perhaps the hardest parting of all is when we gather together at a funeral to take leave of someone whom we have loved for a long time and who has loved us as well. Feelings of numbness, grief, and sadness mark these heartaching and heartbreaking moments. We all know departures only too well.

Yet there is something intriguingly strange and wonderfully different about Jesus' goodbye. Gospel writer Luke tells us that when he withdrew from them, "they worshiped him and returned to Jerusalem with great joy" (Luke 24:52). The disciples have finally come to grasp who Jesus was and is. He is far more than a good prophet of God's reign or a brilliant teacher of God's values. They now know that in the life, death, and resurrection of Jesus, they have encountered the God of the Old Testament in a direct, personal, and firsthand way. Their only adequate response is joyful worship. But now he has to leave them and return to the heavenly realms.

In the desolation and despair of our goodbye moments, let us draw courage from the ascended Christ. There is someone in heaven, available to each of us in our pain, who understands what it means to say goodbye. This is what the disciples now know. This is why they can part from Jesus with joy. His ascension is the final confirmation of his victory over evil and death. He withdraws, but from now on his loving and consoling presence will not be localized to one geographical spot. His living presence is now freely and infinitely available to every human being everywhere through all time. Ascension-shaped Easter people know this and celebrate it, even with the tears of our goodbyes in our eyes.

### *Daily Practice*

Bring to the risen and ascended Christ a recent goodbye. Speak with him about it, share with him your feelings, and listen to what he may say to you. Throughout the day, keep the image of the ascended Christ in your heart.

# ALL

*He who descended*
*is the same one who ascended*
*far above all the heavens,*
*so that he might fill all things.*
**Ephesians 4:10, NRSV**

Right at the outset, let me say that the word *all* really does mean all! Our daily verse invites us to find Christ in everything. Paul tells us that, through Jesus' ascended presence, his Spirit now fills all things, the visible and the invisible, the conscious and the unconscious, the physical and the spiritual. Nothing is exempt from his living presence. He wants to meet us, wherever we are, whatever we are doing, whoever we are with. His glorious reality penetrates and permeates the whole earth.

Everything changes when we build our lives on this biblical conviction. It is within our everyday lives—cooking meals, playing with our children, cleaning the house, going to work, enjoying friendships—that we get to live out our union with the risen and ascended Christ. Through the Spirit, Christ is present with us wherever we are in whatever activity, revealing God's love for us. This is the life-giving insight that Brother Lawrence brings to the world in his wonderful book, *The Practice of the Presence of God.* Brother Lawrence learned to meet God both in the sacraments of the Eucharist and in daily life. Within the midst of our own busy and active lives—provided we are willing to learn how to practice the presence of God—this can be our experience as well.

Some simple steps can get us going along this path of practicing the presence of Christ. We can learn how to regularly turn our minds in a Christward direction throughout the day. Simply repeating the name of Jesus with love and affection is one way to do this. We can choose to remain constantly thankful each day for all the gifts that come our way. Living thankfully nurtures our awareness of the Divine Presence. Above all, we can seek to do everything we do for Christ, offering our daily work to him as our act of living worship. Through simple practices like these, developed into habits over time, we come to know that Christ indeed fills all things.

### *Daily Practice*

Select one way of deepening your awareness of Christ's presence in all things and put it into practice.

# KNEEL

*For this reason I kneel before the Father,*
*from whom every family in heaven and on earth*
*derives its name.*
**Ephesians 3:14-15**

Think about your knees for a moment. Like our ankles, they are important hinge joints in our bodies, but they are far more complicated. People who know about the body tell me that they provide articulation between bones held together by ten ligaments. As you may know from your own experience, when we damage any of these ligaments, it is immensely painful. Our knees make it possible for us to bend our legs.

Today we find Paul bending his knees in humble worship and adoration. What is it that prompts Paul to pay homage like this? Much of the answer to this question lies in the content of the first two chapters of Ephesians. There we come across repeated references to the ministry of the risen and ascended Christ. (See Ephesians 1:3; 1:20-23; 2:6.) Certainly, for Paul, "God exalted [Jesus] to the highest place and gave him the name that is above every name, that at the name of Jesus every knee should bow, in heaven and on earth and under the earth, and every tongue acknowledge that Jesus Christ is Lord, to the glory of God the Father" (Phil. 2:9-11). When last did we bend our knees in adoration and homage? Has our sense of awe and reverence deepened or waned? Are there other hidden idols in our hearts to which we offer our sacrifice of worship?

We kneel in confession and ask for God's mercy in those many times we have broken the heart of God. The Holy Spirit invites us to scan our hearts and to bring our attention to those attitudes and attachments that underlie our unloving, disobedient actions.

Is the Spirit inviting you to bend your knees in renewed love and praise? As you do so, may you realize that the Holy One before whom you bow is your "Abba, father." You can kneel knowing that you are loved, accepted, and forgiven!

### *Daily Practice*

Take time to kneel before the Father today. It may be a time to bend your knees in worship and submission or in confession and penitence.

# FACE

*When Moses came down from Mount Sinai*
*with the two tablets of the covenant law in his hands,*
*he was not aware that his face was radiant*
*because he had spoken with the LORD.*
**Exodus 34:29**

Our faces say a lot about us. They reveal something about our age, our disposition toward life, the pain that we have experienced, the joys we have known, the worries and anxieties that we have, and so much more. We spend large amounts of money on our faces as well. We buy skin-care products like moisturizers, makeup, lipstick, and eyeliners to help us look a little better to others. But what money can never buy is the radiance that the Spirit alone can bring to our faces, no matter how wrinkled or weather-beaten they may have become.

God-given radiance reflects the presence and work of the Holy Spirit in our lives. When we interact with the Lord as Moses did on Mount Sinai, the Spirit begins to work deeply within us. Our characters begin to radiate an inner integrity, an obvious serenity, a loving responsiveness toward others—all of which reveals vividly that we have been with the Lord. Moses' face shines when he comes down from the mountain. It is so bright that people around him ask him to cover it with a veil. Indeed, in Exodus 34:30 we read that they are "afraid to come near him."

The faces of Easter people glow with this inner radiance that the Spirit gives. Can you think of persons you know whose faces have been radiant in this way? The wonderful thing is that, like Moses, they are completely unaware of the glow on their faces. These people remind us that as we remain in conscious relationship with the Lord, the Holy Spirit continues to change us from the inside out. Will it not be something very special if those who look at our faces today think to themselves, *I am sure this person has been with Jesus.*

### *Daily Practice*

When you look in the mirror today, ask the Holy Spirit to make your face shine with the Spirit's presence. Trust that your face will reflect the presence of the Lord with us.

# ROOM

*When [the apostles] arrived,*
*they went upstairs to the room*
*where they were staying.*
**Acts 1:13**

The upper room plays an important role in Jesus' preparation for Pentecost. Almost immediately after his ascension, when the disciples return to Jerusalem, they go to the upper room. It offers them the necessary space where the disciples can pray and wait for the promise Jesus has given them: "You will receive power when the Holy Spirit comes on you" (Acts 1:8). Certainly, we know it also has a special place in their memory because it is the place where Jesus met with them in significant and special ways. Now, as they wait along with the women Christ followers, they want to encounter him anew in the power of his Spirit.

As Pentecost draws nearer, this should be our desire too. As we have seen over and over again in our Eastertide journey so far, the Holy Spirit is the giver of sparkling life that bubbles up within us like an inexhaustible and powerful spring. The Spirit refreshes and renews us for joyful obedience in God's world. Many of us, especially when we constantly are involved in giving to others, find ourselves dried up and exhausted inside. We feel we don't have much more to give. We long for a fresh experience of God's Spirit to give life to our hearts and our bodies. Only then will we be able to truly live as Spirit-empowered Easter people in our broken Good Friday world.

Maybe we too need an upper room where we can wait and pray in preparation for a fresh outpouring of the Spirit. You might remember Jesus once told his disciples that when they pray, they need to go into a room, close the door, and speak to their Father in secret. (See Matthew 6:6.) As we move toward Pentecost, I invite you to do this quite literally. It could cause this Pentecost to be vastly different from all the others. Indeed, it may be the day when the spring of the Spirit turns your life into a deep reservoir from which life-giving streams begin to flow toward others around you.

### *Daily Practice*

Today, find a few minutes to go into your room, close the door, and ask the Father to prepare your heart to receive a fresh outpouring of the Holy Spirit.

# WIND

*Suddenly a sound like the blowing of a violent wind
came from heaven and filled the whole house
where they were sitting.*
**Acts 2:2**

I was born in a South African city fondly known as "the windy city." A day in Port Elizabeth can begin calmly, and then suddenly gale-force winds can take over and rip through the city. From an early age I learned that, while we cannot see the wind, we certainly can experience it. We can listen to the wind with our ears, feel it on our skin, and breathe it through our nostrils. Around us, we see how it moves the grass, bends the trees, stirs up the waves, and blows up the dust. As a child it wasn't long before the wind became something for me that could never be tamed or controlled or manufactured. It was totally free, it could blow whenever and however it wanted, it was completely beyond my power to control, and it certainly was much bigger than I was.

When Luke describes that first Pentecost moment, he compares the coming of the Holy Spirit to the blowing of the wind from heaven. As Tom Wright, the Anglican biblical scholar, makes clear, the whole point of this metaphor is that through the Holy Spirit, some of the creative power of God comes from heaven to earth and does its work right here. Wright writes, "The point is to transform earth with the power of heaven, starting with those parts of 'earth' which consist of the bodies, minds, hearts, and lives of the followers of Jesus."* Pentecost is all about the risen and ascended Christ, now with his Father, blowing his powerful presence into our lives in the here and now.

Easter people always seek to stand in the Wind. When we open our lives to the Holy Spirit, heaven comes to earth, beginning in and with us. The Spirit energizes our bodies, renews our minds, makes our hearts responsive, and gradually transforms our lives. We become aware of the huge difference between walking against the wind and having the wind at our backs. Let us therefore ask the Holy Spirit to blow out the stuffiness and staleness that may be present in our lives right now. Let us also imagine the Wind blowing through our lives, breathing into us a new freshness, cleansing our vision to see more clearly, and empowering us to live as Jesus would if he were in our place.

### Daily Practice

Experiment today with an exercise of the imagination. Sit quietly and in the stillness imagine the Wind of God blowing into every part of your life. What might your life look like?

*Tom Wright, *Acts for Everyone: Part 1* (London: SPCK, 2008), 22.

# FIRE

*[The apostles] saw what seemed to be tongues*
*of fire that separated*
*and came to rest on each of them.*
**Acts 2:3**

What thoughts or images come to your mind when you think of fire? Perhaps you remember standing around a fire, warming yourself on a cold winter's night. You may picture your family sitting together around a fireplace, enjoying good conversation. You may think of a time when a dangerous forest fire was brought under control by the starting of another fire. Or you may recall watching a piece of iron being held in a fire: First, its rust is burned away; then it turns red and then white, until it looks as if it is part of the fire. However you respond, I am sure you will agree that fire is not only something good to be cherished but also something dangerous to be respected.

On the day of Pentecost, the Holy Spirit comes to the early disciples not only as wind but also as fire. What do these tongues of fire resting on each of them represent? Surely, it is an outward sign of what the Holy Spirit is doing inside their lives. Think of the associations we make with fire. Can we not suggest with some confidence that the Pentecost fire represents similar kinds of experiences? Can it be that the fire of God's Spirit is warming cold hearts, joining the family of believers together, bringing sinful tendencies under control, and burning away the rust of iron-hard hearts until they are aflame with the fire of God's love?

I remember a mentor and friend encouraging me "to always guard the fire within." I keep his words close to my heart, and I hope you will too. We need to keep the fire of the Holy Spirit burning within us. Otherwise, our hearts can so easily become lukewarm and grow cold. If that has happened to you, do not be discouraged. There is cause for much hope. Pentecost can happen again for you and me. We can prepare ourselves to ask once again for the burning Spirit of God to come and rest even on us. Do you need another Pentecost this year?

### *Daily Practice*

As a symbol of the fire of the Holy Spirit, light a candle near where you will spend your day. May it remind you through the day that Jesus wants to baptize you with the Holy Spirit and with fire.

# TONGUES

*All of [the apostles] were filled with the Holy Spirit
and began to speak in other tongues
as the Spirit enabled them.*
**Acts 2:4**

The first Pentecost gifted the early disciples with a miracle of communication. When the disciples begin to speak about the amazing things that God has done in Jesus Christ, all people in that diverse and cosmopolitan crowd hear about God's love in their own languages. They do not need a translator to understand. It is a miracle accomplished by the Holy Spirit. This may surprise us. Usually when we think of the gift of tongues, we think of unintelligible sounds and syllables. The Pentecostal experience is different. It is an experience of remarkable connection across the divisive boundaries of race, gender, age, and nation that we so often create.

What could this mean for us? Especially in diverse contexts, we yearn to communicate the good news of God's never-giving-up love in a way that others will understand. That communication means so much more than just getting across some information about Jesus to someone else. Instead, it involves us in the miracle of communication whereby the Holy Spirit makes known through and beyond our words the reality of Jesus Christ to the people we are with. This miracle echoes the experience of the early disciples from that first Pentecost. Without their being caught up in a movement of the Holy Spirit, those disciples would have been unable to effectively communicate Christ to others.

I long for this gift. I long to be able to communicate the availability of Jesus' love, grace, and mercy in the tongues of those around me: in the tongues of teenagers and pensioners and all those in-between, in the tongues of the beaten and the broken and the battered, in the tongues of the rich and the famous and the privileged, in the tongues of the overemployed and the unemployed and the underemployed, in the tongues of the lonely and the rejected and the ostracized, and in the tongues of the sick and the bereaved and the dying. The opportunity to share Christ is endless. If this is your longing too, join me today in asking for a greater measure of the gift of the Holy Spirit who alone can bring about the miracle of communication.

### *Daily Practice*

Consecrate your tongue to God today. Ask that your tongue may be baptized with the Holy Spirit so that it may be conformed to Christ and converted to his ministry of loving words.

# SAW

*[The apostles] saw what seemed to be tongues of fire*
*that separated and came to rest on each of them.*
**Acts 2:3**

Yesterday we explored the Pentecostal miracle of communication into which God's Spirit invites us. It is the invitation to speak of God's endless mercy and great goodness in the tongues of people around us so that they may understand the good news. Let us look today at how we can get more involved in this divine miracle. I want to suggest that this miracle of communication helps us see others in a clearer and deeper way. In a deep sense this is what happens for those early disciples. The Holy Spirit makes possible a fresh awareness of other people and, as a result, they can communicate more effectively.

The Holy Spirit continues to do this today. As John V. Taylor has said, "The Holy Spirit is the invisible third party who stands between me and the other, making us mutually aware."* When we become more aware of the persons next to us, their joys and their sorrows, we are far more sensitive to how best to speak about God's good news. There can be no genuine mission and ministry without this eye-opening change, made possible by the Spirit. Strikingly, in the first miracle recorded after Pentecost, "a new way of seeing" plays a big role. When Peter heals a man crippled from birth, we read: "Peter looked straight at him, as did John. Then Peter said, 'Look at us!'" (Acts 3:4).

*John V. Taylor, *The Go-Between God: The Holy Spirit and the Christian Mission* (Eugene, OR: Wipf and Stock Publishers, 2014), 19.

Perhaps the one word that describes this Spirit-given awareness is *empathy*. There is a great need for empathy today. Our children need more than only to be brought up; they long to be seen by their parents. Our elderly need more than a cup of tea; they need to be recognized in their uniqueness. Our unbelieving friends need more than for us to share the good news with them; they long to be accepted and valued for who they are. As we grow in empathy toward others, we find that we are better able to communicate with them. Indeed, we begin to speak in the tongues of those around us, no matter how different they may be.

### *Daily Practice*

Ask God's Spirit to help you truly see those around you today.

# ASK

*"If you then, though you are evil,*
*know how to give good gifts to your children,*
*how much more will your Father in heaven*
*give the Holy Spirit to those who ask him!"*
**Luke 11:13**

Asking is at the heart of our interaction with God. There is a good reason for this. Although God really wants to give good gifts to us, God will never force them on us. I am sure you have noticed from your own experience that God is seldom pushy. God always respects our freedom and waits for us to ask. Nothing is automatic about the way our relationship with God operates. Not surprisingly, throughout the Gospels, Jesus often speaks about the importance of asking. For example, the Lord's Prayer is made up of requests that Jesus invites us to make our own. (See Matthew 6:9-13.)

Today's verse invites us to ask the Father for the gift of the Holy Spirit. Hopefully, by now we have seen how important it is for us to be filled with God's Spirit if we want to live faithfully as Easter people. We cannot operate effectively out of our own resources and wisdom. We need to experience more of the Holy Spirit in our lives. Jesus makes it clear that his Abba, Father in heaven wants to give the Holy Spirit to us. In this regard, God's lavish generosity far exceeds our own as parents, who know what it means to give good gifts to our children. Still, God waits for us to ask.

In our asking, we need to come to the Father simply, vulnerably, and honestly. You can begin where you are, right now. Maybe you feel you have come to the end of your own resources and need strength from beyond yourself; maybe you are tired of simply going through the motions in your faith, and you long for a sense of immediacy in your connection with God; maybe your Christianity has become a cold, ethical system, and you deeply want something that is more personal and intimate. Wherever you are in your journey of faith, there is always more of God's Spirit to be experienced. Easter people know this, for we are a Spirit-empowered people!

### *Daily Practice*

Meditate on these words: "How much more will your Father in heaven give the Holy Spirit to those who ask him" (Luke 11:13). Receive them today as an invitation from God for you to ask. Respond to God's invitation by making a simple request from your heart for the gift of the Holy Spirit. Ask and receive in Jesus' name!

# PENTECOST

*When the day of Pentecost came,*
*[the apostles] were all together in one place.*
**Acts 2:1**

Today is the day of Pentecost! You may want to read through the second chapter of Acts again. On that day the disciples receives God's power from above. It is a power that enables them to go out and out-live, out-think, and out-love the ancient world. They receive something extra, something new, something they did not have before. They receive power in their hearts. The flames of fire and the sound of wind are just outward signs that the Holy Spirit has been given to them. They receive what all of us desperately need: the Spirit of God filling us and helping us overcome the evil within and around us.

We need to face the simple fact that to try to follow Jesus without the Pentecostal power of the Holy Spirit doesn't work. We just cannot do it. From a biblical point of view, it appears that everything that happens before Pentecost is a preparation for this gift of Wind and Fire. This world was created so that in following Jesus Christ, we can have friendship with Abba. Father and be given the Holy Spirit. God-made-flesh lived, died, and rose so that our eyes would be opened to the unfathomable depths of God's love and we would be ready to receive God's Spirit. The message of Pentecost is that there is a new power available, the very power of the kingdom of heaven.

So can I invite you again to think deeply about the place of the Spirit of God in your life? Is the Spirit of God really at work in your life? Are you experiencing greater freedom in your walk with Christ? Are you growing in your capacity to love in the way that Jesus loved? Do you have some sense of God working through your words and actions? Perhaps you can reflect on these questions when you gather together in one place with other followers of Christ for worship. This is what the early disciples did on that first Pentecost. Pentecost happened for them together. This could also be your experience today as you join together with other Easter people to celebrate the outpouring of the Holy Spirit on the church. Whatever it is that you decide to do today, few things are more crucial in the life of faith than remaining open and yielded to the Spirit of God. Easter people are a Spirit-empowered people!

### *Daily Practice*

Consider worshiping today with God's people in a local congregation near you to celebrate the gift of the Holy Spirit.